Designed by Flowerpot Press in Franklin, TN.
www.FlowerpotPress.com
Designer: Jonas Fearon Bell
Editor: Johannah Gilman Paiva
PAB-0808-0138
ISBN: 978-1-4867-0831-4
Made in China/Fabriqué en Chine

Copyright © 2017 Flowerpot Press,
a Division of Kamalu LLC, Franklin, TN, U.S.A.
and Flowerpot Children's Press, Inc., Oakville, ON, Canada.
All rights reserved. No part of this publication may be
reproduced, stored in a retrieval system or transmitted,
in any form or by any means, electronic, mechanical,
photocopying, recording, optical scan, or otherwise,
without the prior written permission of the copyright holder.

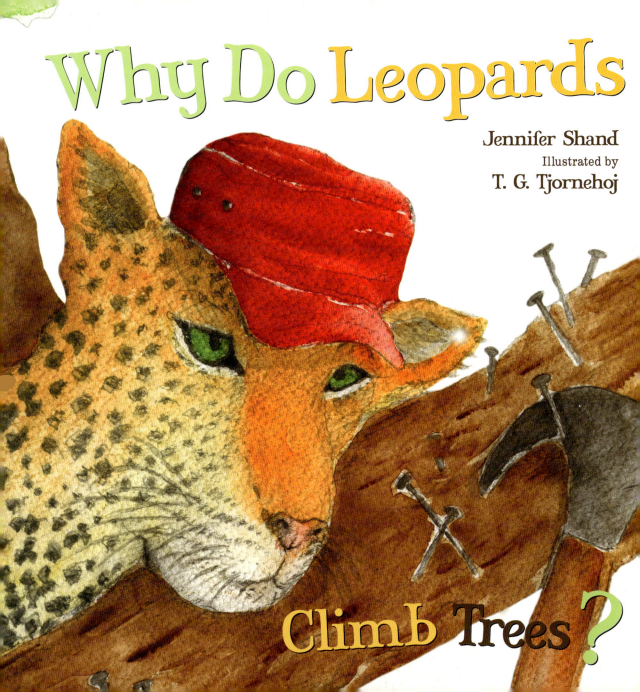

How do animals survive in the rainforest?
The rainforest is very humid and it rains an extraordinary amount. There are many animals that live there, so there is competition for food. Each animal must have something special about them to live there.

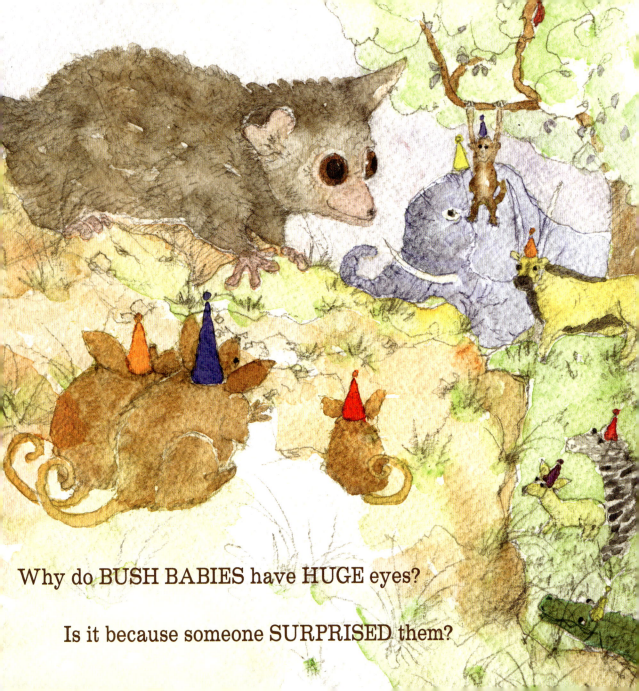

Why do BUSH BABIES have HUGE eyes?

Is it because someone SURPRISED them?

Bush babies have huge eyes because they are nocturnal, which means they are awake and active at night instead of the day. They have large, round eyes to be able to see at night! With their big eyes, they can find food easily and move around safely in the dark, while other animals are asleep.

No, that's silly!

Anteaters have very long tongues because their food is often hard to reach. They use their tongue to reach inside an anthill or termite mound to get the insects out! Then, they swallow the bugs whole before they get a chance to sting!

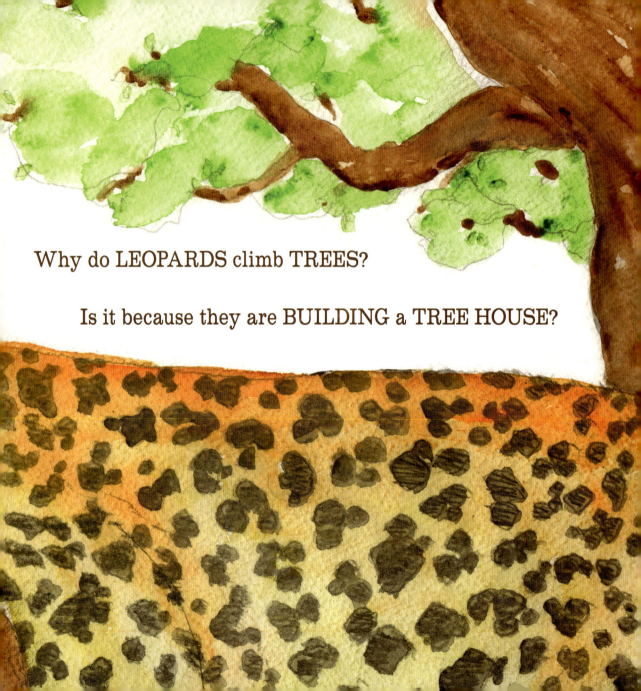

Why do LEOPARDS climb TREES?

Is it because they are BUILDING a TREE HOUSE?

Leopards climb trees and rest on branches because it is safer there since it is up high and their spots blend in with the leaves. They also take their food into the trees to keep it away from other animals that might try to take it away from them.

Why does the FLYING DRAGON LIZARD have a FLAT body?

Is it because it was accidently SAT ON by a GORILLA?

No, that's silly!

The flying dragon lizard has a flat body because this makes gliding through the air faster and easier! Having a flat body is more aerodynamic, which means the wind and air move around its body better. The flying dragon lizard actually does not fly, but glides from tree to tree, and this keeps it off the ground and away from predators.

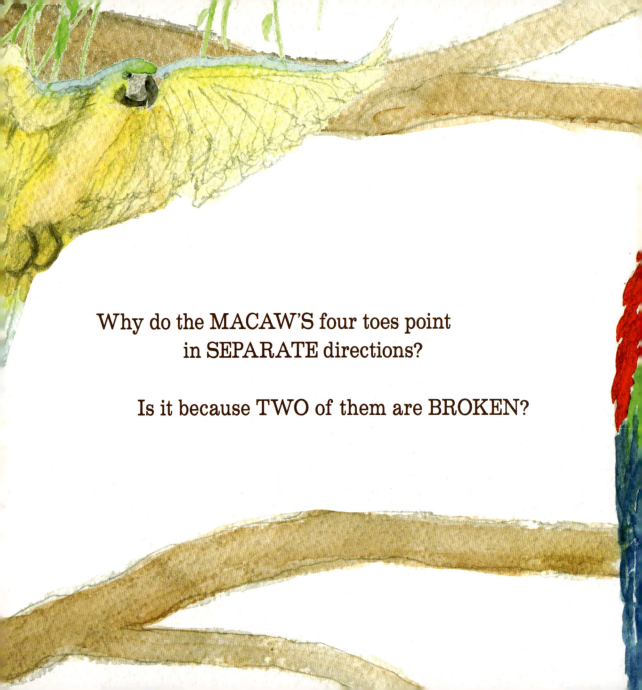

Why do the MACAW'S four toes point in SEPARATE directions?

Is it because TWO of them are BROKEN?

No, that's silly!

Macaws have two toes that point forward and two that point backward because this makes their grip very strong! It allows them to hold on to tree branches as well as their food. (When you do not have hands, a foot like this is very helpful for eating food!)

The animals in the rainforest sometimes do funny things or have funny features, but it is all so they can survive there. The rainforest is a very important part of the world and many animals live there. In fact, more plants and animals live in the rainforest than anywhere else on Earth! The rainforest is not only the home of many animals, it is also the home of many trees that clean the air and provide the oxygen we breathe. This makes it very important to take care of the rainforest and all of its trees!